What I Did
Not Tell You

What I Did Not Tell You

by
Ken Wheatcroft-Pardue

First Printing: 2020

ISBN: 978-1-7350976-0-2
(Hungry Buzzard Press)

Published by:

Hungry Buzzard Press
P.O Box 80164
Keller, TX 76248-2300

Front cover photo courtesy of Emma Cary

Acknowledgements

"What a Thing to See," *Oak Bend Review*.

"La Isla de Malhado," "Lost," "Weeding the Family Plot," and "A Thousand Moons," *Texas Poetry Calendar* (various years).

"A Memory of Water," *Main Channel Voices*.

"Living and Dying in Real Time" and "My Mother's Problem," *The Texas Observer*.

"Life in the Sad City" and "What I Did Not Tell You," *Borderlands*.

"This Happiness," "Cicatrix," "Those Old Fans of My Youth," "Bedbugs," "Revenge Fantasies, "Ken the Obscure," "At 10," "Always Lost," "Hitchhiking in Wisconsin, May 1979," "7/7/77," "A Poet Died Yesterday," and "Insomnia Poem #23," *Ilya's Honey*.

"What Are You?" *Barbaric Yawp*.

"The Day She Couldn't Use the Phone," "The Bad Year," "Stop Reading this Poem!" "Ode to the Sluts of Yesteryear," "An Old Fart Remembers," "In Front of La Gare de Lyon," "Big Grandma," "The Peaceable Fridge," "Bray Auto Parts (Houston, Texas, circa 1976)" "The Year I Stopped Enjoying Seeing My Wife Naked," "Love Song for the Terminally Maladjusted," "My Wife's Ashes," "I Find it Strangely Comforting," "All Backs Wear Out," "Woe to Those Poets of Easy Comfort!" "In Jackson 5: My Wife's Last Birthday (April 28, 2015)," "Everything is Lost," "At 50," and "Just a Slice (June 1976)," *Red River Review*.

"A Face in the Window," *Blind Man's Rainbow*.

"Dante in the Divine Comedy," *Pitchfork*.

"Revelation on a Plain Jar," (now called "Revelation") and "The Cost of Empire," *poetsagainstthewar.org*.

"A New Theory on the Dynamics of Moving Bodies," *Taproot Literary Review*.

"Mexican Bus," *Anthology*.

"Seeds," *Concho River Review*.

"Hot!," "My Mother," and "Tales of Hoffman," *Maverick Press*.

"Lost Bodies," *California Quarterly*.

"Something Unspoken," *Touchstone*.

"In Real Life," "Negative Space," "Genealogy," and "I Miss," *Wilderness House Literary Review*.

"Walking Through Chinatown, June, 1976," *My Favorite Bullet*.

"The Memphis Bus Station August 1980,""The Rust That Runs in our Blood," and "Family Lore," *Ginosko Literary Journal*.

"about:home," "Nowhere Near," "When You're a Kid," "Setting," and "Our Old Bodies," *Front Porch Review*.

"The Blue Guitarist" and "It Is What It Is," *The Blue Lake Review*.

"Some Errant Clouds," *Bolts of Silk*.

"Visiting My Mom (1966)" "Global Warming," "A Fire: Galveston, 1965," "Teacher Daymare #254," "This Morning," and "July 4, 2017, *Amarillo Bay*.

"This Fire," *Nerve Cowboy*.

for Marianne

Contents

Postcards

A Fire: Galveston, 1965 15
Visiting My Mom (1966) 16
In Front of La Gare de Lyon 17
Bray Auto Parts (Houston, Texas, circa 1976) 18
Walking Through Chinatown, June, 1976 19
Just a Slice (June 1976) 20
7/7/77 21
Mexican Bus (April 1978) 22
Hitchhiking in Wisconsin, May 1979 23
The Memphis Bus Station, August 1980 24
In Jackson 5: My Wife's Last Birthday (April 28, 2015) 25

What Are You?

What Are You? 29
Stop Reading This Poem! 30
The Bad Year 32
Lost Bodies 33
Dante in the Divine Comedy 34
The Day She Couldn't Reach the Phone 35
Life in the Sad City 36
At 10 37
Genealogy 38
Our old bodies 39
Setting 40

La Isla de Malhado

La Isla de Malhado 43
Lost 45
My Mother 46
Weeding the Family Plot 47
Those old fans of my youth 48
Always Lost 49
My Mother's Problem 51
A Memory of Water 52

Family Lore 53
When You're a Kid 54
This Fire 56

Living and Dying in Real Time

Living and Dying in Real Time 61
A poet died yesterday 62
A New Theory on the Dynamics of Moving Bodies 63
Something Unspoken 64
Ode to the Sluts of Yesteryear 65
Tales of Hoffman 66
Negative Space 68
Everything is Lost 69
July 4, 2017 70
I miss 71
I find it strangely comforting 72

A Face in the Window

A Face in the Window 75
A Thousand Moons 79
Revenge Fantasies 80
What I Did Not Tell You 82
The Year I Stopped Enjoying Seeing My Wife Naked 84
Big Grandma 85
about:home 87
Nowhere Near 88
Cicatrix 89
Global Warming 90
My Wife's Ashes Are in a Box 91

The Rust That Runs in Our Blood

The Rust that Runs in Our Blood 95
This morning 96
Hot! 97
Revelation 98
The Cost of Empire 99
It is What it is 100
The Blue Guitarist 101
Some Errant Clouds 102
Insomnia Poem #23 103

Woe to Those Poets of Easy Comfort! 104
Teacher Daymare #254 105

This Happiness

This happiness 109
Seeds 110
The Peaceable Fridge 111
In real life 112
An Old Fart Remembers 113
Bedbugs 114
¿Quién sabe?) *114*
All Backs Wear Out. 116
At 50 117
What a Thing to See 119
Ken the Obscure 120
Love Song for the Terminally Maladjusted 121

About the Author

122

Postcards

A Fire: Galveston, 1965

On my grandma's stoop, we watch
a fireman carry a black man fireman-style.
The burned man's skin hangs from his arms
like the fringe on the leather jackets
I lust for this summer of 1965.

Then my grandmother stands up,
shakes her head,
No sympathy, she spits out.

That idget smoked and fell asleep.
He deserves to die.
He put everybody in danger
and didn't give a good god damn.

I notice how when she shakes her head,
the loose skin under her chin flaps like a lizard's.
Then she clears her throat and lets fly a wad of phlegm.

With open-mouthed awe, I watch its wobbly trajectory
as it arcs over my head, somersaulting through the air
until it plops in the sand, yards away.

As the ambulance's siren slips out of ear shot,
the burned man's wife returns.
And somehow recognizes
the waterlogged blackened mattress as theirs.

Bending over it, she screams, then breaks for the door.
Grim-faced men in white dress shirts hold her back.
She claws at them,
screaming in a high-pitched voice
something incomprehensible
that sounds like jagged glass.

Visiting My Mom (1966)

At the crack of dawn,
us kids play possum,
so daddy has to carry us
to the brimful Falcon in our pj's.

Now reeking of Aqua Velva,
we cuddle in blankets
on the green vinyl bench seats.
"Awake" to a car filled with smoke
from Folgers, Winston, Lucky Strike.

Make good time through towns that echo
some unnameable, unknowable past:
Prairie View, Hempstead, Brenham, Giddings, Elgin.

Finally, Austin – the State Hospital
is huge, wooden, white-planked,
like something straight out of *Gone with the Wind*
with screened-in porches
where from the outside you can hear
the insane stomping their feet,
not once, but continually,
as if pounding out messages
in Morse Code
to their imaginary friends
hovering somewhere nearby.

I even spot a few jitterbugging,
swinging their invisible partners behind them.
And from a dark corner one poor soul howls,
the sound of the purest human despair,
the saddest music I'd ever heard.

In Front of *La Gare de Lyon*
(Paris, France, August 1974)

Sur la avenue au coucher du soleil,
streetlamps pop on in sequence,
while Citroëns and Renaults
stream into traffic circles
barely escaping connubial conflagration
by American inches.

At 17, I flip through a dog-eared copy
of Somerset Maugham's *The Razor's Edge*,
lent me by a Frenchman,
inexplicably fluent in 50's hipcat English.

In *la Champs Élysées*,
he presses the flesh to Daddy-Os,
trolls for cranked dollies,
a Lucky Strike always dangling
from his James Dean sneer.

I read the first page –
I have never begun a novel
with more misgiving. –
smile then plunge into a sea of words.

11-point Palatino Linotype, to be precise,
filled with Gold-bug Speedsters, raccoon coats,
shaved-head Buddhists, and flappers galore.

I learned then in front of *La Gare de Lyon:*
while streaming through our teeming time,
all of us exist in the now,
but also at the same time
in one parallel universe
after another, after another, after another.

Bray Auto Parts (Houston, Texas, circa 1976)

On the long, long counter sit three black
Delco ashtrays – already at 10 brimful with
cheap cigars, bent cigarettes, gray ashes.

Go-Jo's pumice smell permeates the air.
Along with thick layers of dust & oil-caked heads –
Mopar, Chevys, Buicks, Fords: all are equal here.

Tailpipes hang mute from the ceiling
like Calder's mobiles. Sparks fly
as I clean an oil-encrusted valve.

A phone call, a mechanic
needing a water pump.
When? *Last week would've worked.*

I thumb through a humongous catalogue,
jot down the number, grab the box,
make out the sales slip, and run to the Green Monster,

a half ton '72 Chevy. Blast off!
CB radio spewing its staticy argot.
My arm cooled by the side window
positioned just so.

Walking Through Chinatown, June, 1976

My pupils dilate, my heart rate climbs.
Too many days, living off peanut butter
and Aunt Jemima syrup sandwiches.
Glucose, dextrose, fructose,
"the building blocks of life,"
coarse through my veins.

Sounds – Mandarin's tonal staircase,
the pop and sizzle of sesame oil in charred woks,
an old couple's shared laughter –
come alive.

As do smells – pungent leeks,
whiffs of jasmine,
a dark cloud of diesel,
a fistful of crackling wonton.

On Telegraph Hill,
I spot the perfect couple, rich and oblivious,
arm and arm,
like some credit card commercial.

At sunset my worn-to-the-cork desert boots
give up the ghost.
I stand there.
My stomach empty.
My room, too damn far.

Just a Slice (June 1976)

5 hours in the blistered sun
trying to hitch a ride out of Alamogordo –
pasty-faced seniors in Winnebagos for some odd reason

not trusting my long-haired bearded self –
I gave up. Called my old man
to wire me bus fare.

In Amarillo I had an hour layover,
walked the main drag
at 10, one crazy Saturday night.

All these teen angels, cruising, revving their engines,
honking their horns. Wide-eyed girls, their heads
hanging out the windows, shopping for boys.

While the boys in tight Wranglers leaned against their cars,
coolly eyeing only *las chicas lindas.*
Red cherries shining in their palmed hands,

surreptitious Lone Stars expertly held
under fender wells by index fingers.
Hormone levels and sexual tensions

hit all-time highs.
Just a tiny slice of Americana.
Could John Adams have conceived it thus?

7/7/77

Head fake, sweating, dribbling,
turn-around, jump, fadeaway, rim shot.
Our tennies scuffing the ill-lit half court,

breathing in thick slices of noxious Union Carbide air.
A viscous night lit only by the refinery flares almost perfect blue light.
The rainbow of effluent in the ditches,

a hunk of bacon hanging on a string, crawdad bait.
The exploding cumulus,
the sweet and pungent smells of honeysuckle and oleander.

As we walked down West Grey one summer evening,
across the street, ballet dancers
practiced twirling without getting dizzy.

Running down West Beach, the waning moon
over her soft shoulders, the curl of black waves,
the wet sand, the feel of lips and tongues.

The causeway's halogen lights,
the smudge of moon on the bay,
the cooling air on our taut wet skin.

Mexican Bus (April 1978)

Azure-bodied, white-topped, it chugs down *La Calle Leyva*,
scattering a bevy of boys, two ragtag teams of soccer,
as the driver stutters a rosary at his copilot, *la Virgen*.
Above the rearview mirror, she shines golden rays
into the souls of the lost and smiles like a well-meaning *tía*

just over my head at the just-budding teens, in their crisp
blues and whites, refugees from the nuns' harsh discipline.
Their minds on *cuerpos*, not a corpse,
on everything but the sagging body of Christ.
First their whites and blues brush, but soon they grind,
and the wet fullness of lip and tongue
that passes all understanding
becomes their sacrament.

Aroused they are blind to all, especially me,
just another *gringo loco*, searching for the waters of Lethe,
swimming in the mescal of forgetfulness,
diving into the tequila of solitude,
to forget how her voice and mine
were sucked into those icicled telephone lines.

Now I am silent as the rats that scatter as we pass *el palacio de Cortes*.
At night they nibble on the bones of *Aztecas* and Spanish *cabelleros*.
I'm one with both tribes.
For if it meant eternal life, I'd cut out the heart of another
and hold it still beating into the face of the sun.
and if it meant riches, I'd sell my own mother for a map
to El Dorado's *caminos de oros*.

I'd do it, I say, as the brass band plays in *el zócalo*,
and Swiss twins, blond and sexually experienced
(5.5 partners by the age of 19),
sip *Negra Modelo*
waiting for me.
Yes, *carpe diem*, I'd say,
if I could only get up.

Hitchhiking in Wisconsin, May 1979

As a '62 Electra skids to a stop,
I pile into the back seat,
backpack and all.

Against the opposite corner,
a teenaged girl is scrunched up.
Her thin knees pressed against her flat chest.

She's a dishwater blond with pigtails,
wearing candy-striped short shorts
with a pink halter top.

Something seems off about her,
from her purple toenails to her vacant eyes.
Perhaps, it's the translucent quality of her pale skin.

Or maybe it's that even though
she's heavily lipsticked, mascaraed, and rouged,
she looks all of 14.

We're headed to Hollywood,
offers the driver with no prompting.
I'm off to make my fortune.

Then turns around in his seat,
points at the girl,
She's my Publisher's Clearing House, my Lotto Jackpot.

The girl then takes out a Donald Duck Pez
from her tight pockets
and pops one into her wet, young mouth.

The last time I saw her was at a rest area in Wisconsin.
The driver was helping her
into the passenger side of a semi.

I could just barely
make out the trucker,
a white cap on a big gut.

The Memphis Bus Station, August 1980

wasn't much of a sanctuary, really –
more like a phantasmagoria of the grotesque,
society's riff-raffs – losers, lonely hearts, small-time grifters,
the habitually unemployed, dope-peddlers,
opening their raincoats to expose,
not their genitalia,

but plastic sealed bags
filled with only the best Mexican thunderfuck,
a choice of papers (yellow and white),
and a colorful cornucopia of pills
of one sort or another,

all of this staged
with the background music of videogame aliens
being annihilated,
slowly, deliberately,
combined with those oh-so-subtle undertones
of the tinny sound of coin-operated TV's.

In Jackson 5: My Wife's Last Birthday (April 28, 2015)

In the psyche ward's
cafeteria, she sits,
picks at her food.

Her brow, wrinkled
like a hieroglyph
translated: unbelievable suffering.

Then cutters, schizos, manics,
substance abusers gather
to form a rag-tag choir.

Belt out an off-key
Happy Birthday to you
to someone they don't even know.

My eyes flit from face to face.
Whatever private hells
they're going through

(and there must be many)
look far
faraway.

If I'd seen them outside
I'd figured these young,
good looking people

hadn't a care in the world.
Tears flow.
I can't help it.

And when they finish,
I cut two small pieces of cake for us.
Then tell these blessed nut-jobs
the rest is theirs.
And thank, thank, thank them.
Only wish I could've given them more, much more.

What Are You?

What Are You?

One in six billion, special, are you?
Got a bit of education – a degree here,
another one, there.
Speak a foreign tongue, you say.
My, my.

Oh, two, but both poorly.
Written here, been rejected there.
Had a few lovers – the sniffling, cold kind
that come at midnight teary-eyed to your window.
But none of those boom-boom nymphs
à la prime time with swimmer's thighs.

Well, I don't think they exist either,
or if they do, not for long.
Inside each beauty is a fat matron
clucking her tongue against her lobster-fed cheeks,
planning yet another shopping trip
to browse third world capitals
for only the best bargains.

While you and I,
we'll be lucky to get out of town this summer,
yet, I guess, lucky nevertheless
to be two in 6 billion.

Stop Reading This Poem!

Stop reading this poem!
It will take 36 1/3 days off your life.
I guarantee it!

Stop reading this poem!
It will not get you tenure.
And most certainly won't get you ahead.

What did I say?
Stop reading this poem!

It will not raise the Gross Domestic Product
1/1000 of a scintilla of an iota.
It cures nothing.
In fact, it is guaranteed to produce hair loss.

Don't read this poem!
It's already too long and doesn't even rhyme.

Do not read this poem!
It will neither tighten your ass nor tan your skin.
And it will never make your teeth pearly white.

If you read this poem,
your underarms will not stay dry,
and you will never become popular
with those who snubbed you when you were young.

Do not read this poem!
You were confused when you started,
and, look at you, you're still confused.

This poem does not illuminate,
nor does it eliminate unhappiness.

In fact, it just might cause you to curve off your beaten path,
to drive – just drive away from what was once your life
so steeped in habit you long ago stopped noticing
how the world like shrink wrap had contracted around you.

You see, it's just a poem,
but if you've read this far:
Start over!

The Bad Year

In the bad year,
that no one will speak of ever again,
the walls were blue & words meant nothing.
People would talk & it'd come out like puffs
of dank & dirty smoke.
And no one could look anyone in the eye.

The media were filled – as always –
with beautiful lies that no one,
I repeat, no one believed.

Dogs did not bark.
Birds refused to sing.
It was as if the world were a cartoon
& the artist, maybe because of lack of time
or, why not, just plain laziness,
had forgotten to add color
& those magic cloud-like balloons.

Lost Bodies

There are decaying bodies left in ditches
by mercurial, stubble-faced hitchhikers
with snub-nosed pliers sticking out
of the back pockets of their Wranglers.
The howling barking dogs know it.

There are old women, who dining alone,
imagine company and talk to their blurred faces
in the lime-stained reflections of spoons.

Who would glory in this wilderness of alienation?

Last night I saw two lovers
fighting in the Safeway parking lot.
Their passion cracked passing headlights.
It embarrassed me, making me stutter
to myself in my rear-view mirror.

Every morning I read the criminal blotter.
I know every perversion's fundament by heart.
At night I count them
like closed-eyed, black-faced sheep
and sleep dreamless,
coiling
in my unmade bed.

Dante in the Divine Comedy

At life's midpoint, Dante's road forked
from the straight and narrow & he ended up
in the Divine Comedy, a second-tier
whorehouse on the outskirts of Venice.
What a bright and lively place it was!

There he'd paw one bored whore after another,
naming one breast Ghibelline, the other, Guelph,
he longed to unite Italy with his tongue.
They didn't mind though, the three kinds of girls there:
the leopards, the lions, and the she-wolves.

Dante was partial to the leopards
But sometimes he'd try the lions
But never the she-wolves,
They smell like the pit of hell, he'd always say,
like sulfur on dry cankers.

But, ah, recalling those halcyon days
brings a shape to mind,
in fact, many shapes.
Their very memory keeps
the bitterness of death at bay.

The Day She Couldn't Reach the Phone

Autumn and the mysterious cylindrical rumble of leaves,
unfettered by the cornucopia of symbology,
only the scrape of orange, yellow, red on the drive,
while inside there's only the immortality of dust.

The kitchen phone hangs by its cord,
twisted in an aria.
Her body, prone, but still breathing,
reaches but cannot quite hang on.

Heavy breathing, a puddle of sweat, a pool of urine,
staining her flowered skirt,
searing pain twitching from hip to skull,
while a recording repeats,
You must now hang up.

The slow chaos aging brings,
the sure evaporation of an order beyond love.

Life in the Sad City

I grew up in a sad city
of wet streets, dour faces,
lining musty halls without end,
while the thick air
stagnant from sour smells
rose from between guttered grates.

Imagine, just imagine, Romeo and Juliet,
not as two love-struck teens forever frozen
in high school-English-class amber
but two middle-aged, overweight
ex-to the zillionth time-lovers,
foes till death do thee part.

That was our life in the sad city,
so sad, even butterflies
killed themselves,
diving into the daily maelstrom
of chrome grills.

Everyday the sun
that bleached the grass
burned us,
staled the very air
we breathed.

Even the mockingbirds,
bored out of their gourds
with their wretched songs,
happily crashed
into the glass buildings of transnationals
as a finger of cirrus gilded the evening sky
and cars screamed by,
as if traffic were not individual cars
but a single organism
with a manic heart and raving brain.

At 10

The world is wet.
In front of our round faces,
water droplets swirl,
while my little sister and I trudge on.

From her wood-paneled
Country Club station wagon,
a neighbor lady asks
Y'all want a ride to school today?

For her, I suppose, just trying to help out
what must've seemed
like the two almost waif-like children
of the crazy woman down the street
who very nearly burnt her house down.

For me: the mist dropping –
the opposite of bubbles rising
round and full drops,
bounce off lobed leaves, then tumble
toward us, a glint of light
passes through their thin membranes,
to plop on the root-kicked up,
uneven sidewalk between us.

Then a squint of my eye;
a quick shake of my head.
We trod on, my sister and me.

Call it pride; we did.
Though truth be told,
it was pretty damn close to shame.

Genealogy

Our ancestors were lovers.
They scratched at lace, tore bodices,
ripped flannel, beds buckled, frames collapsed.

And don't you know, it was a civic act.
You couldn't very well hide
heavy breathing in one room, could you?

Our ancestors were killers.
Their sharp bayonets found the soft skin
under countless ribs.

They hacked arms, shot at shadows,
the black powder dyeing their hands,
while someone else's blood
stained their leggings.

And what are we,
but left with this dross,
this accidental concoction,
this all-too-heady brew of ardor
mixed with equal parts brutality?

Our old bodies

speak in syncopated rhythm.
Slow, steady,
then uptempo,
almost out of control,
until
a crescendo.

Then a slow wailing
sax caroms
through curtains
around pastel walls
as we hold
each other
close, close, close.

Setting

What is place?
Touch it – it is the hole in my heart
where sneakers echoed between brick and oleander,
the fecund smell of swerving ditch,
and at dusk, the rainbow of effluent
floating on its surface.

It was the sky every afternoon
filling with the Gulf's humidity,
until the clouds burst
and steam rose from the streets.

It was the honeysuckles
that hung like sagging crosses.
How we stopped to pull
one green, wet stem after another,
till we sucked them all to the last.

What is time?
The ticking of a watch,
the whisper of digital,
the sidelong glance of girl,
resembling someone we knew —
what was it? — 40 years ago now?

It is the slow
hardening of our hearts,
our memories slowly leaking,
staining all we see,
the slow shriveling,
shrinking of our lives.

La Isla de Malhado

La Isla de Malhado
The Great Storm
September 1900
Galveston, Texas

After midnight, the dead dance limp as jellyfish.
And with them — pieces of houses – a porch railing, a cornice,
And more: well buckets, branches, whole trees, bay horses,
junkyard dogs, glass bottles, spittoons, round pucks of horse ma-
nure tumbling end over end, a sign advertising Gold Dust Cleaner
(Nothing but water is needed!).

The next day, houses are piled upon houses,
decaying bodies inside.
Their arms hooked around loved ones, if any
or objects – a stitched pillow, a porcelain doll,
a photograph in a gilded frame.

Some still alive cry to be rescued
from the water-drenched insides of homes,
swept blocks and blocks,
then crashed together like playthings
of a petulant, borderline mad God.

At dawn, on the now-naked wind-blown branches,
strange fruit, the dead, every stitch of clothes ripped from them,
in every kind of position imaginable,
the sun tanning their dead skins.
Their carcasses bloom like flowers;
the gulls getting their first taste of human flesh.

Schools of bloated corpses go out with the tides,
washing ashore again and again.
Funeral pyres burn all over the island.
Bodies are stacked like cords of wood
one on top of another.

And the smell – the sweet incense of body gristle
rises into the air.
The flames, a sure sign,
Galveston has shed its modern skin
to take back its old Spanish name –
la isla de Malhado,
the isle of misfortune,
the island of doom.

Lost

They lived near Live Oak in an old house
where the white paint battered by the constant wind
flecked into the red dust that coated their black Buick.

They were distant relatives,
ancient as Charlie Chaplin ambling in silence
across grainy black and white celluloid.

Before supper I lay on their bed
that reeked of camphor and mothballs,
and gazed at the photo of a soldier on their nightstand,
his lips set close together, the flag draped behind him.
They told me he was their son,
that he'd been lost on the battlefield.

After supper, behind their house, I played
the photographed soldier, wandering forever lost
on some deserted battlefield
that had now grown inexplicably quiet.

Like me being lost in the grocery store,
he was still lost,
humming, *Over There,*
wanting to know,
Where's Mommy?
Where's Daddy?
Which way to the exit doors?

My Mother

My mother had a hidden disconnect in her brain.
She'd pull the plug at Christmas
or any damn time she pleased.

She'd light matches in the attic.
Punched them into the white fibers of insulation.
Laughed when I told her to stop.

Danced and chanted incantations
while shaking Kraft Parmesan cheese
on her wrists and scratch them both raw.

In her spiked heeled boots, she clippity-clopped
through one red-tiled mall after another,
charging our family into deepest debt.

And in her spare time,
she free-wrote a secret life of sin and betrayal.
Blared her radio past midnight to drown the voices.

Finally ended up in a padded cell
with time to wait for cigarettes
doled out for good behavior.

An easy escape for someone
with an imagination.
An easy life, really.

Weeding the Family Plot

Something in your genes
that sets your office hands
to feeling dirt.

That sets your heart
on the rusted tendrils
of barbed wire.

Waiting for a cloud's fist,
waiting for a south wind.

My ancestors prayed for rain
in their years of drought,
prayed for the abolition of debts,
the souls of the dying.

Paid no attention to their brown skin
coated with a fine red dust
and furrowed on the back of their necks.

Just like the lizards
that crawl with certain impunity
on their aging headstones.

Those old fans of my youth

made with forged and tempered steel
(spilling its white phosphorescence
in a sooty Pittsburgh circa 1965)
with those propeller-shaped blades
that were sharp enough
to chop our little digits plum off,
just as well as any white-aproned butcher,
on blood-stained sawdust,
meaty fingers wrapped around his dripping cleaver.

Our blood would surely spurt out
like an untapped oil derrick,
Spindletop, all over again,
and just as sure, all our female
relatives – the oddest assortment of married and spinster aunts,
grandmas and cousins twice removed – would faint
at the sight of our fingerless hands.

And, then, of course, where would we be
with no fingers to dial the operator?
And shouldn't we have thought about that
before we did what we oughtn't?

Always Lost

In that first full moon,
I noted how their labyrinthine tattoos
snaked across their nude bodies.

I could not help but notice
their foul smell – a mixture
of alligator fat and dirt
slathered across their towering bodies
to keep at bay
the hovering clouds of mosquitoes
that haunt these beaches.

But now hunched with them
on this leeward slope of dune,
I, Núñez Cabeza de Vaca,
also wear nothing.
When in Rome . . .

Now *los indios*, the Capoques,
are dying of a sickness
that infects the stomach.

Nothing stays down.
One orifice or another
works overtime till death,
like sweet mercy, comes.

Ridiculously, I am their *curandero*.
Endlessly I mix herbs I do not know,
try my best to comfort the lucky dying.

Bow my head,
recite a *Pater Noster,*
and for good measure
throw in an *Ave Maria.*

But did any *milagros* follow me
on the green waves
I rolled in on?

Every day I pray to God
I'm not murdered in my sleep,
a jagged knife across my gullet
in this strange land where I am always lost.

My Mother's Problem

This is how it works:
words fill up with helium
until they float away,
the hard ones first:
agoraphobia, schizophrenia,
manic episodes, denial.
They float so gently away
you hardly notice them gone.

Then come the so-so words –
toilet, dentures, roast, fondue,
gleam, press, iron, tumble dry.
Finally, the rest line up –
boarding passes ready, ETA decided.

It's not like what they say –
the words being on the tip of your tongue.
They're always floating
just over your outstretched hands
and you, always so short.

Then, even words like:
walk, run, laugh, I, you, cry, love, me.

There you are,
steeping in a wordless void
filled with white noise,
a kind of silence,
which wouldn't be half bad
if you could only remember
who you were and are
and who is that strange man
hunched over the paper
in the kitchen nook
holding a wash rag filled with ice
on a gash
just above his swollen eyes?

A Memory of Water

I've seen the receding chin,
the disappearing hair, the moles
that grow to molehills.
Who needs a crystal ball?

Right now my mother's staring into space,
not recognizing the walls,
not recognizing a face.
Water pouring onto the floor.

Father, hunkered down, his usual position,
wades into this pool of despair,
more concretely, the water
Mother's spilled onto the floor
that's spread to the floorboards,
laps against the oven.

The only ripple is my father's shuffle
that you'd think might stir up something,
a memory of water,
summers at Stuart Beach, Lake Mead, childbirth,
but nothing,
damn it,
nothing shows in her face.

Family Lore

Genes are like germs
that never go away.

That sentimental sop –
we never really die –
is proved true, once again.

Why there's Uncle Tom's alcoholism
popping up in grandkids & great nephews,
& Aunt Etta's schizophrenia, ditto,

showing up decades
after she dressed herself in her Sunday finest,
duct-taped her windows and doors,
then stuck her head
into her brand new Magic Chef.

As Saint Disney says,
in the magic circle of life,
nothing really dies.
Amen.

When You're a Kid

1.

Ten-year-old me,
doodling on school books unopened,
bored to tears.

Overhead fluorescent lights abuzz,
the constant electric hum,
and always a phalanx of those huge Figurematic

Smith Corona adding machines.
Yet another tax office in April; my father
with three kids and a sick wife, always working an extra job.

2.

That smell: eons of dust and beach sand mixed with concrete floor.
In the back room of my grandma's dry cleaners,
clouds of steam rise,

while the pressman's sweat
rains down on clothes, concrete,
the old metal steam cleaner, every where.

My sisters and I play tag,
dodge between, even under
newly dry-cleaned Sunday suits.

3.

Jukebox music & greasy fry smell gloriously
intertwine in the all-night cafe air.
My other grandma waitresses,

pinballing back & forth from booth to kitchen
again & again. Bored, (ah, there must be a pattern here)
I shoot ice cubes on the Formica table

with its grooved aluminum edge & boomerangs
inside boomerangs. My sisters, their patience long spent,
tattle. Who can blame them, really?

This Fire

Kicking up oyster shell dust, two shit-kickers
skid off the Farm to Market.
Wanna ride? one shouts out his window.

OK, I say.
In the cab: *We are a couple of high mothers,*
Quaalude crazies.

Cranks up an 8-track *Stairway to Heaven,*
suddenly jags off the road.
In the headlights' glare, I watch

as they tear down
somebody's wooden fence.
Gonna be a big bonfire tonight, man.

Drugs and pussy, all night, all night.
Their sodden mouths open;
their voices bend the windshield.

I shrug, climb out the cab,
help stack the planks.
On West Beach, we discover their tribe.

They grab wood willy nilly,
then pitch it on a fire, nearly high as three men.
Their shadows dance.

The flames, too,
a Saint Vitus dance,
drugged pyromania, surely.

I escape down the beach.
Soon my hair is wet with mist.
So soaked, drops rain from my beard.

Cold moist breath of smoke,
of a fire, somewhere. There. Right there,
(Is it real?)

I sit on my hams, rubbing my skin.
This fire.
This fire.

This fire.

Living and Dying
in Real Time

Living and Dying in Real Time

I flip a page. Anna Karenina has yet to find a train
suitable for suicide. While less romantically,
in the 21st century,
I'm stuck flying in a converted sardine can.

On my right, my daughter dozes.
Over her shoulder, a low bank of clouds
spreads like icing, but more:
whole cloudscapes of mesas and canyons bubble up,
while furrowed ridges stack on top of each other
like a Hindu Kush hiding some celestial Shangri-La.

And below us, the Mississippi River –
and as I write those 3 words
visions of elementary school spelling bees dance in my head –
winds its sure way past rednecks and metrosexuals.
Ah, at last, an equal opportunity river.

I glance at my grown daughter: tall, beautiful, blond,
best piece of work I ever did.
Though I broke a sweat, as I recall,
it didn't take long before her mother unstraddled me
and was off to work.

I was passed out on the bed,
dreaming of flying,
the clouds spread out
like a tussled bedsheet.

A poet died yesterday

a prize-winning, fairly famous poet, in fact.
If ever a Nobel Prize is given posthumously
for assholishness in literature,
this guy should win hands down.

Back in the Seventies, he visited my college
to give a few readings,
make a good payout,
maybe even get laid.

The *literati* from my small college
schlepped him to a Tex-Mex joint, where he,
too busy gossiping with some hanger-on
from the Ivy League, tuned us out.

Then, at his request,
we hauled him to a liquor store,
where he bought enough bottles of hooch
to knock out an elephant, maybe two.

The next day, red-eyed, word-slurring,
obviously hungover as hell,
he gave a reading – of sorts.
After three questions in a scheduled Q&A,

and a pause no more than a nanosecond,
blurted, *So if that's all, I'm gone.*
Then Mr. Big Name Poet walked out,
as he did life, yesterday.

A New Theory on the Dynamics of Moving Bodies

Forget Einstein.
Time is no relative.

Let all the light bulbs shine.
Who cares how quick light moves.

Our bodies are the sweetest equation.

Tear off the sheets!
We've no time to be tangled.

Tonight, let's experiment
on the dynamics of our moving bodies.

I hypothesize:
our mass plus our motion
will square all roots,
split every atom,
and never, ever bomb.

Something Unspoken

I was there behind the window,
behind the Venetian blinds, cringing
like a little boy hiding from his father's belt.
While you were down there,
there near the fountain looking up at me,
though you could not have seen me.

Your eyes or maybe those shadows that cup the eyes like hands,
Perhaps they saw me,
and reached out to hold these scarred cheeks.
Again, we are in the same orbit.
Again, nothing really means very much to me.

I lie draped across your bed like a forgotten coat or tie,
as you dodge in and out of the mirror.
While in every backyard in suburbia
mutts rage back and forth to bark at dark clouds
that threaten to explode but really at nothing.

Even they know it is something unspoken,
like the shadows that twitch behind your eyes,
even as you stretch in the full-view mirror.

Ode to the Sluts of Yesteryear

I miss you.

I miss your halter tops, your faded hip huggers,
your flowery leather belts.
I miss even the salty taste
of mid-afternoon sweat above your lips.

Yet most of all, I miss
your gymnastic tongue that once danced
between my inner lip and bicuspids.

Really, I miss you.
Where are you now?
Are you bitter?

Having sworn off men,
having sworn off women,
& for what?

Cable & comfort food?
Chocolates & channel surfing?
The nightly ride on the La-Z-Boy?

Or, are you still interested?
Your muscular tongue still hiding
behind those Mona Lisa lips.

Tales of Hoffman

1. Hoffman's Complaint: Wrong, Again

No coof am I, but faradized I am the theodolite and vernier of
all things.
Free as any American coot,
my life has been like riding a pump jack drunk.
But I was sure as any logic has illogic,
sure as every something has nothing,
that the reason we were born with two legs & two arms
is so we could hold onto someone while we ran.

2. Hoffman's First: Love's Pain

With a lipectomy and collection of cream liqueurs,
she was every trendy lover's dream.
(But later he'd concede she was all too real.)
Hoffman's first love was fixed with money.
Plastic surgeons adored her.
Her kissable breasts were two bobbing silicone delights.
And orthoed, her bone white ivories in perpetual pearly smile
locked nearly always at just that wrong moment.

3. Hoffman in Love: For the Last Time

Hoffman had been told by those in the know
that the only thing that lasted forever was herpes,
and that the tension level in American middle class, college-
educated marriages
had been tested to be ten parts per thousand, which was
dangerously high.

But this did not stop Hoffman. Instead of work, in care of her
husband he wrote.
Under stacks of bureaucratese he hid scrawled notes.
Certain words, like: coughing, confusion, hair, husband, rain
were inadvertently circled by coffee rings.
And those brown O's circled into that night.

She was crying and lovemaking
and even her black hair (birdnest/bush/savior) smelled of rain.
But now Monday morning he slumps
at his gray government-issue desk in another city.
No one notices how he nurses her cold.
It rests closed-eyed and fetal bent,
swinging with its tiny pink hands (more like claws)
on the inner arches of his ribs.

.... gs disappear:
That candle, smelling of vanilla,
we once lit,
the round mouth over our heads,
the eyes that squinted abstractly,
both gone for good.
Even that old wreck we once drove
is now being driven by another.

Yes, copulation once thrived in the back seat,
where now a child stares out the window,
eyes like two cat's eye marbles,
yet another refugee
from the cruelty of playgrounds.

Now another drives it.
The hands that grip the wheel, perhaps, grip iron,
bending it into shapes,
but, more likely, has fingers rawed red
from pushing buttons
on some frigging keyboard all day.

By rush hour, the boredom,
the utter disgust of work
weighs on his temples,
presses against the closed windows,
bending them, outward,
slowly, almost imperceptibly,
until they burst.
Pellets of blue-green glass spray
onto the hot burning blacktop.

Everything is Lost

Me, the dumbest sentimentalist of all times.
Today I've been thinking on that run-down apartment
house my grandma lived in near downtown decades ago.

Been razed for years, but today
that musty smell in the hallway came back to me.
Is there even one other who remembers that?

And the dents my grandma put in the ceiling
with her broom when the Mexicans upstairs
made the walls shake with their *conjunto*.

Today, I'm even weepy about her white Dr. Scholl's,
her True Detective magazines scattered near her bed,
watching Divorce Court on a TV with rabbit ears akimbo.

My sisters and I'd eat on a fold-out
card table in the living room: fried chicken,
butter beans, cornbread in a cold glass of milk.

In the back, an alternative universe
of peeling paint, glass-strewn alleys,
old men parked on their back stoops curling Colt 45s.

Everything is of a time,
and in time,
everything is lost.

4, 2017

V, Bogie in a trenchcoat is paused
exactly between knowing and not knowing.

While outside fireworks pop
in the daylight's last gleaming.

10 years ago, on the Redneck Riviera,
my wife and I watched

the Gulf reflect rockets' red trails,
spider webs of explosions.

Ohhs and ahhs wafted between waves,
as embers slowly floated toward their end.

After burgers and wine, we made love.
a couple long-knowing each other's just right spots.

Later we lay in bed. Curtains opened,
half asleep, our breathing in sync.

Two hearts surely beating as…
An unhinged locust squalls.

Exactly two years ago she died.
Her pictures are here and there.

I do not cry –
well, much, anymore.

I miss

our goofy life together.
Cheap dates, free museums,
our bookish, old movies life.

I miss someone to laugh with,
while out getting an afternoon buzz
from espresso shots and chocolate, lots of it.

I miss our homemade cards,
always years behind the tech curve,
coupon-clipping life.

I miss you taking forever to pick your entrees,
dancing with you in the kitchen barefoot,
your laughter when I sang off key – always.

I miss our foster dogs
romping in the living room,
homemade napkins, old sit-com life.

I miss you next to me,
your smile always steadying me.
I miss our silly, goofy life together.

it strangely comforting

ome patch of dust
on that hard-to-get-to shelf yonder
could be dead skin cells
sloughed off
her bent, pain-racked body
more than 2 years ago now.

Or that some microbial creature
still spirals
through my twisted, maze-like intestines,
a parting gift from her,
one last kiss,
that last time
we shared bodily fluids.

A Face in the Window

A Face in the Window

1.

Summer: the smell of decay,
the pink mimosa flowers that twist my heart
in the dark place where the roots have died.

Summer: this morning
while I was still in bed,
outside my window mimosa leaves
flap like magpies' wings
looking down on its prey.

Summer: Now, this night,
in the alley, I bathe
in the warm moon.
The smell of honeysuckle
wraps its loins around me.

I sigh then go for a walk
to the railroad tracks then back.

When the evening is thick, there is a face
wrapped in her concentration.
I saw her in a dream last winter.
She was sitting on the snow
selling bottles of water from Lethe.

2.

If she could, she would have looked inside
to see herself. How the naked light bulb
above the sink cast a strange glow upon her.

But she was there at the kitchen window,
picking up each plastic plate
from the gray water.

Her grandmother had given them to her
on that night before the flood,
the one she and Lynda had gotten stuck in,
with the brown, rain-swelled, septic tank
smelling water gurgling, through the air vents
of that old Ford they had then.
Gurgling onto the clear plastic mats,
onto Lynda's bare feet and her blue tennis shoes.

She remembered carrying Lynda.
The brown thigh-deep water rubbing
along the white cement incline,
where wet rats, shaking their ash-colored fur,
barked like squirrels.

She remembered:
the smell of the snuff, the sight of the train engineer
passing over head,
with his brown-stained mouth wide open.

It made her shake to remember:
the cottonmouth twisted on a fallen branch.
But that was how many years ago?
She didn't know, but before grandma died.

She lifted her face to the black window,
red tail lights swimming through her reflection.
She thought:
cars have beating hearts, not just piston and rods,
spark plugs and gas.

Her husband laughed at her for this.
She did not hate him for that.
Today was his day off.
He had gone to visit his mother in the nursing home
and then to the cemetery.

She didn't like the cemetery:
Too many artificial flowers.
And the nursing home?

It smelled of the bile of rotting old men.
It made her think:
of the rats and the snake.

She finished the last dish, the last cup, the last pan.
Then she washed her hands in tap water,
then taking the sponge,
dragged it across the black-topped oven.
Smoke rose.
She watched it for the longest.

Then she put back the sponge,
wiped her hands on her ample bottom.
She wondered:
When will my husband be home?
It was getting late.

3.

A train whistle echoes like jazz chords,
vibrating between trembling leaves
through locked doors and closed windows,
and there you are,
looking in,
or perhaps, you walk by.
Because it's late, very late.

But instead you stop in a puddle of broken glass.
With one piece stuck to your shoe you finally
lift your feet from the view of the window.

What did you see?
What is it that made you stop,
then look at your companion,
if you have one,
and shrug those toothpick shoulders,
cracking them,
sending goose pimples down
your companion's spinal cord?

But you say you are alone,
and that as far as you can see
all that inhabits the street
is one stray, rat-colored cat,
rubbing up against a street lamp.

But you never notice the cat
because you're looking at the woman in the window.
At her eyes that never meet yours,
but eyes you see just the same.

A Thousand Moons

I remember what was there:
Patterson's Grocery, the old man's filling station
and the Ritz, its marquee long shattered, even then.

When it was summer,
we rocked on the porch.
Steam rose from the gutters,

and whenever we walked
we walked in the shade, and at night
a thousand moons would burn upon a thousand windows.

Nothing I have is mine.
When I was a child
I thought the fields and ditches, even sounds –

Grandma driving her flatbed up the gravel drive,
and the wind pressing the loins of weeping willow
against my window – were mine and mine alone.
But that is not the way it is.

Revenge Fantasies

1.

You are fit and trim, 20 pounds lighter. Your smile,
your 100-watt smile beams. Every woman,
especially the young ones, cannot help themselves.
They sigh and cross their legs.
She is there. You know it.
You walk by her as if she were a table.
Tears collect at the corners of her eyes.

2.

She is in the hospital. Her life ebbing away
and only a transfusion of your blood can save her.
But – unfortunately – you are too busy.
Your sock drawer needs rearranging,
and all your books simply must be organized.
Alphabetically or by subject, this time?
We'll just have to see…

3.

Her head's impact has birthed a glassy spider web
on her windshield. Blood trickles
out of her unconscious mouth,
as steam rises from her busted radiator.
You drive by the scene, carefully weaving
around puddles of broken glass.

You go for your cell, ready, indeed willing,
to forget your pain, but, on the other hand,
you've heard it's unsafe to call while driving,
maybe even against the law.
Oh well, your mind wanders and miles on
when you remember, you shrug.
Surely somebody's called by now.

4.

Children and time – those 2 thieves – have robbed her
of her beauty. She waddles through the mall,
sweating in the air condition, even her breathing labored.
You ease past her, not saying a word, but frowning
to show your displeasure of having to pass another fat cow.
You wonder, haven't these people heard of
vegetables, exercise, restraint?

What I Did Not Tell You

1.

At the yellow house on our street –
the one where the son once sold crack
out of his converted garage window,
his driveway like a drivethru,

a couple weeks into your hospital stay,
his sister wandered off from bathing her 10-month old.
Maybe to text someone,
or to bitch about how absolutely bored

to tears she was,
or just to stream a movie, *quien sabe?*
To cut to the quick,
the 10-month old drowned
in a tiny bit of soapy water.

The paramedics tried, but no.
All the family stood in their front yard
of hard dirt and high weeds –
and wailed and wailed.

2.

It truly sucks to get old.
Our family doctor, around my age,
was going through something.

Dyed the gray out of his hair,
shaved his mustache,
pumped iron in earnest.

Even I noticed. Surreptitiously,
I checked his wedding band.
Still on, but just barely.

You see, he texted our 28-year old daughter,
nothing gross, no pics of his package,
just an "innocent" invite to coffee.

While you were splayed out
on yet another hospital bed,
I phoned him from your bathroom.

When I told him he lost us as patients,
he started crying, honest-to-God tears,
telling me how sorry he was

doing this when he knew
how afraid I was for you.
I will never forgive him those tears.

The Year I Stopped Enjoying Seeing My Wife Naked

I flinch when I see her arms now
bent and thin as where you grip a bat.
Her fingers once so soft
are now bent like bare branches

after a winter storm,
swollen at the joints
like knots on a tree.
Slowly mutating with each passing year,
more and more Dafne-esque.

Hard to imagine her
as she once was, a sylph.
Honestly it takes all of me,
though even then sometimes I can't.

A picture in my mind: Inks Lake, 1985,
a woman hurt by another man,
looks up at me.
I free fall into her eyes,
deep and malachite.

Big Grandma

Big Grandma, we called her because she was, well, big,
standing there in full waitress regalia.
Ah, that familiar plop of her white Dr. Scholl's.
Her green Falcon, like some minnow, swimming
across Fannin past the old ice house.

Clank of horseshoes, thrown beer bottles smashed,
Dirty men scratching their loose khaki crotches,
wads of tobacco puffing their red blood-vessel popped cheeks.

While my sisters and I, across the street,
bathed in the sweet choking smell of mimosa,
pink bursts helicoptering through asterisks
of skitters' body heat in the still azure, circa 1967.

If angry, she'd call us, or try.
Bobby, Jibber, Sugie, she'd stammer,
naming her own kids with a grandkid
(always the wrong one) thrown in.

In the nursing home, after her third stroke,
I gave her a brief recital of her life.
*You were born in Georgia. Your brother's name
was Tobe Peet. Your sons were...*
everyday, again and again. Till finally it caught.

Then one night my father clutched me in his arms.
My mother is dead, he croaked
Then collapsed in my arms.

The smartass in me wanted to say,
And this is a surprise?
But I held him up instead.

Once she held my hand, as we breathed in wafts
of bus-spewed diesel in downtown Houston.
She with red-dyed beehive, me, my blond prone-to-cowlick hair
slicked back with palms-full of Vaseline.

Guiding me below the street, like the anti-Beatrice,
to paradise – a basement cafeteria
with Doric columns, gold-leaf walls, yeasty roll smell,
organ music played by a lady with pink hair
that matched her pink harlequin glasses.
Yes, the closest thing to heaven on earth.

about:home

It was in a meadow,
so as better to see
the sun's rays
drop like golden honey
on its homey
Good Housekeeping Seal effervescence.

Inside a woman with make-up,
with hose, in a dress
in high heels, for godsakes!
is vacuuming
the most perfect
unlived-in-looking living room.

It's dark & dim.
My grandmother waddles
down the hall to the back bedroom –
her portable TV babbling Divorce Court,
a bottle of Milk of Amnesia,
sits on the bedstand
on top of a lace doily
next to the unmade bed.

It was built in 1946,
in the post World War II housing boom,
used good wood with straight, plumb lines,
real wooden cabinets.

Leapfrogging in the wet grass,
blades upon blades
stuck to our legs.
Clutching a handful of china berries,
we ducked behind perfect corners.

Nowhere Near

(In memory of Janis H.)

Sticky, sweaty, Houston hot –
summer of '77.
We biked on trails, until two boys
in banana-seat bikes veered

and your peddle caught one of theirs.
Behind you, I watched
as you flipped, spun into the air,
then landed – plop! – beside the trail.

When I got to you, you couldn't stop laughing.
I bent, kissed your beaded-with-sweat lips,
and congratulated you
on the best bike wreck ever!

December '81:
Shadows played on the far wall,
while on the phone, droned
a voice so irritatingly calm.

In the semi-dark, I sat
on my-then girlfriend's bed,
in a relationship that I knew even then
was ebbing towards its end.

Over the phone,
the mundane details of your death.
Where: in Swaziland, a Peace Corps volunteer.
How: a single-vehicle accident.

Some truck you'd hitched a ride with
had a blow out, and you were thrown from the bed.
Janis, you fell into the African sky.
but this time I was nowhere near.

Cicatrix

The old man's scar was huge, jagged like
some callow kid's crude drawing

with those thick elementary school pencils,
a lightning bolt on the chest of the hero.

In fact, so damn nasty looking
it made me flinch.

I tried my best not to look.
Brought up religion, politics,

everything my mother told me not to.
Anything that was not the scar

that tugged my eyes
out of their middle-aged lethargy.

The next day when I woke
in a room full of citrus smells,

and the brightness of primary colors,
I realized what I should've known,

what I should've admitted long ago:
the total, the complete impossibility of love.

Global Warming

I'm like the moon,
orbiting you,
a prisoner of your gravity.

Slowly I circle your equator,
brushing against your lush tropics,
fingering the wetness of your Panama Canal.

Then curl around the swollen belly of your Africa,
until I wake to nuzzle
in the moist forgetfulness of your Pacific Trough.

My tongue flits,
explores every inlet,
every cove.

My mission: to warm you
pole to pole, to melt your glacier,
your deep, your hidden icebergs.

To free you from your Fortress of Solitude,
your do-it-yourself cloister. To free you
from your enemy: your too, too reticent self.

My Wife's Ashes Are in a Box

On the box are:
1. her wire-rimmed bifocals
2. her flip-up sunglasses
3. my wedding ring

After she died, all I had to do
was get a side-long glance
of that box

and the lights would go jagged.
Strange. But I miss bawling like that now,
and today, I'm missing her so much.

Her goofy, sweet, sidelong smile.
Her warm body curled up next to mine.
I'm beyond tired of skittish women

in their fifties, who always overshare
that once they were promiscuous,
but, just my luck, not anymore.

They're wary. Me, not so much,
I just want someone fun
who's not afraid of her own shadow.

The Rust That Runs
in Our Blood

The Rust that Runs in Our Blood

Tufts of yellowed weeds sprawl from behind barbed wire,
limed with ferric oxide that slowly rots.
While all around, in the sodden chill,
plump faces smile that uniquely blank smile.

Belief in all manner of hokum is as numerous
as the number of angels dancing on a pin's head –
a virgin giving birth to a God-child amidst the ammonia
and methane of a barn, whole hosts of celestial beings,
all inexplicably blond, even every sparrow's feathers
is worthy of debate. Are they a God-send or curse?

Ah yes, here even the end-time con is writ large.
Yet go past the bend, past the stripped and fallen billboard,
past the ravine of abandoned cars to Rosa's,
where after hours the city fathers let down what's left of their hair.

After whisky shots, they wink and smile at all the saps
who buy their recycled for-the-zillionth-time piety –
like some *dance macabre*, skeletons stripped by the cawing buzzards,
their beaks red with blood, their eyes unfocused and blank
amidst their daily bread of lies, their agile conformity,
their well-deserved self-hatred.

This morning

eating my 4-minute eggs, my 2 veggie sausages, my whole-
                                                    wheat toast,
out my front window, a passing school bus's rumblings
launch a jumble of wings.

Our annual spring rite in full swing.
When cedar waxwings swarm on my holly bush
to gorge on its red berries.

Like Hitchcock's *The Birds,*
an ear-full of them, their beaks
spotted with scarlet drops, swoop down.

My eggs cold, my plate abandoned.
I stand at the window, eyes flitting from branch to branch,
at this orgy, this blood-red frenzy.

Hot!

It's known by all the whites, at least,
that all the illegals will be fired –
maybe not today, not even tomorrow
but damn sure before payday.

They're there – like lambs being led
to slaughter, sweating in their masks,
squatting in their squalor.
Their black lenses reflecting
white arcs from welder's wands.

They say if you stare into that light
you go blind and everyone –
your wife, even you own mother –
will leave you by the road
off some farm to market,
where even the good people litter
because no one cares.

And you'll sit there alone, a speck.
Not even worthy of the flies buzzing
in front of your eyes,
just like something you'd flick off your pants
without a thought.

The east wind finally picks up,
that you can feel,
but the lightning that arcs across the blackened firmament
you can only wait to hear.

Revelation

I reject the poor school and the rich school!
I reject the humble parish and the First Baptist Church
complete with basketball court, indoor pool, and spa.

I reject television and any snobbishness about television.
I reject the Cineplex, iPods, reality TV,
cable news, and talk radio, especially talk radio.
I reject all who believe sexuality equals identity
and positive thinking rivals wisdom.

I reject all conversations dealing
with exercise, carcinogens, portfolios.
And I strongly reject
potato salad without mustard and pickles.

I reject the fat cows of Bashan,
dressed in their designer sweat suits
grazing the aisles for low-fat foods,
while their daughters with frizzed hair
eye grocery clerks.

I reject the state and all its "isms,"
its snooping, murdering, lying ways.

And I affirm memory and love as sacred.
Not some relics, artifacts, some "things"
to be made use of by well-paid pimps
selling worthless crap!

The Cost of Empire

Tonight our missiles are falling on some village somewhere,
and you, you're not a bad sort.
Sure, like most of us, you're an easily distractible blob,
but you've a heart;

you'd care about this little snippet of news
between the commercials on hemorrhoids and gas
if you weren't so damn busy entertaining yourself
– as it turns out – to death.

For the next week on a business trip
to some godforsaken hellhole,
you shouldn't have been surprised
when instead of trinkets the natives tossed you a bomb.

And when your flag-draped casket returns
without much of you in it,
the President will appropriately get choked up,
just in time for the evening news.

Plus, your wife will look quite fetching in black,
and even your kids will look reasonably well behaved,
stashing their Game Boys in their coat pockets for a few minutes.

Then a few more missiles will fly at a cost of several million each,
while no one will bother to utter the names of the real murderers
in their dark suits and perfectly coifed hair.
No, no one will even think of it.

It is What it is

I've worn down an even half dozen of carpets
to threadbare, churchmouse thickness,
proctoring, urging, mentoring, cajoling
my charges,
largely in underfunded schools
where students who work at all-night
fast food dives,
then hopped up on Red Bull's buzz
sleepwalk through the day
but always – even if they're mathematically challenged —
profoundly aware
of the uneven odds
life, that bastard, has dealt them.

Fact: Nobody picks their parents.
If they did, we'd all pick super models and movie stars,
pro athletes, the mega rich,
not our real parents,
that short, fat, ignorant couple over yonder,
totally void of any fashion sense,
just regular folk
with no money
and even fewer possibilities.

The Blue Guitarist

He's a singer without a song.
Last night his notes
packed up and flew
under the metal door.

But he caught one, a clef note —
held on to its crooked pig-like tail,
and one of its trembling curves
for the longest.

After awhile
it too slipt out of his butterfingers
to shoot into the great beyond.

Words, too, have left him.
No longer are they the protoplasmic,
malleable, life-giving stuff
of once upon a time.

Now they stand,
though sometimes recline,
bored, mute sculptures,
stuffed anachronisms
of an era dying,
perhaps, already dead.

Some Errant Clouds

Some errant clouds scud along the sky,
While their shadows glide along the topography
over hills, malls, rivers, ghettos, burbs.

My blinking eyes, catch this scene.
But between my ears, I wonder . . .
why the hell is this so special?

Same damn clouds as 10, 20, 30, or a millennium ago.
White cumulus with just a streak of blue
racing, patches of azure between them.

So why am I staring, my feet stuck, my neck craning
up at this moveable, ever malleable sky?

Insomnia Poem #23

What you notice in old movies
is that on a voyage,
cigarettes, telegrams,
champagne glasses, darling,
even dead bodies
are tossed overboard
as if the Atlantic
were nothing but a very huge,
very wet trash bag.

And that while our heroes are indeed
filthy rich, they are never ever snobs.
For they call the ever-friendly
and servile help by their first names,
even inquire of their children.

But do you ever notice the help
never calls them by their first names
because they know who butters their bread
and are never fooled
even for a moment,
even on some backlot,
even on celluloid?

For the simple reason,
that when you're the help
you can never afford
to be fooled by appearances.

Woe to Those Poets of Easy Comfort!

Weekends in Connecticut,
chipper didacts, trust fund babies,
who live in cities but write of "nature,"
not as anyone who knows it sees it,
but as a kind of gentrified ecosystem.
Survival of the cutesy!

Woe to those poets of easy comfort!
May they wander for 4 times 10 years,
taking circuitous routes among quiet strangers,
while plagues of locusts
and insurance agents haunt them!

May they be cursed
with unflattering Facebook pictures
and boring, straight-laced children,
who will study engineering
and become life-long Republicans!

Woe to those poets of easy comfort!
May some unnamed Deity
visit their iniquity on their children
unto the third and fourth generation!

And may their words squirm from them
and hide in dark, maze-like corridors,
to be found by true poets
who are always at home in darkness!

Teacher Daymare #254

I always imagine him turning at the door,
looking for all the world
like the star of his own gangsta video,
aiming his gold-plated Glock
straight at my heart.

He shoots,
and I know
you're not supposed to
ever die in your dreams,
but, I'm sorry if my dreams don't comport
with your narrow conception of reality.

For there I am
bleeding on the linoleum
between a trashcan and file cabinet,
a tall stack of ungraded papers
waterfalling
on top of me.

And my students?
Too busy taking selfies,
playing games,
listening to music
to ever anachronistically dial
9-1-1.

This Happiness

This happiness

is so new.
It is like our first born
in her third-hand crib.
How that first month worry
brought us to our knees
to peer through pockmarked slats.

We held our breaths,
till her ribs rose and flexed.
Then holding each other's hands
through the darkened hall
we made our way
to our bed
to try our luck again.

Seeds

I could say
everything that once meant life
means death.

But how goldenrod, bluebonnet,
and Indian paintbrush seeds
convoy around cattail
in the ditch along the Farm to Market,
where I wander erroneous as a clown.

But how after supper I walk,
mistaking the seeds' shining
for reflections of stars,

But how the river will suck the ditch dry,
to leave the seeds
to become ribbons of wildflowers
that will return the spring to me.

The Peaceable Fridge

Do not fret.
Leave the refrigerator to its own devices.
The celery will not war with the carrots.
The milks – both soy and 1% –
will lie quietly as two proverbial lambs.

The Chinese take-out will not hop
from its box to fight the Vietnamese pho.
Nor will the American cheese carpet bomb
the baba ganoush.

Mustard will live next to mayonnaise.
Peanut butter next to tahini.
And the moldy will dwell next to the fresh
and all will be at peace.

In real life

this cold morning, in line
waiting for my daily jolt of caffeine,
I catch sight of this bum
prying his scabbed mouth from Styrofoam.

His face, beatific in coffee smoke,
reminds me of those 12th century
portraits of martyred saints,
calm blue eyes
squinting through a bric-a-brac of skin.

With the swoop of plastic,
the 21st century interrupts.
And I beat a quick retreat
past oil-spots,
wadded-up fast food trash
to my rusty crate
to do by habit
what I've done for years:
drive on, drive on, drive on.

An Old Fart Remembers

You call this rain?
You probably call a mild case of heartburn love.
When I was young, it really rained.
40 days and 40 nights!

We didn't mess with no dinky ark neither.
We'd wade right in,
water moccasins brushing against our thighs,
and for fun we hunted alligator gar with our bare hands.

Once, I even found an Idaho potato,
floating in slime.
After I sidearmed it, it skipped,
skipped for hours like a hyperactive king on a checkerboard.

It didn't stop at no horizon neither.
It just flew right off the edge of the earth
until it hit the sun, and all the water froze.
So we bent some old tin cans and made ice skates.

And skated to the end of the world.
Hell, we didn't have ten trillion TV channels, smartphones,
digital streaming, or any of that modern crap,
but – believe it or not – our lives were still worth living.

Bedbugs

1.
For the record, I did not let the bedbugs bite.
Those bloodsuckers did their bedbug best,
without me nodding acquiescence.

Attracted by our entwined warmth,
in pre-dawn haze, they pierced our skins
with two hollow tubes.
One, to numb us;
the other — to mainline our blood.
Little vampires!

2.
When lifting the box springs,
I saw their teeming city.
Forget sex on the bed.
There was sex in the bed.
A whole bug empire built on their sex
and our blood.

3.
Traumatic insemination – males piercing females
with hypodermic John Henrys,
Imagine ejaculating anywhere,
no orifices, right into their hard body cavities.
(Evolved because of prissy, cold-hearted lady bedbugs,
or because males were just too loutish to bring flowers?
¿Quién sabe?)

4.
But if you think about it,
The wife and I were the real interlopers.
We only slept in the bed.
But it was their home, their Gotham,
their teeming Manhattan.
No wonder they bit their hosts.

5.

But soon the exterminator
will come *à la* Gary Cooper at noon
and nuke the little buggers.
But I will pray for their pint-sized souls
to escape the bonds of buggy purgatory,
just so their hard bodies never return

Backs Wear Out.

All those beautiful women
in their twenties
with their naked, supple bodies,

incredible pre-sagging,
pre-kids breasts,
buns, still firm and shapely,

and well-muscled thighs
wrapped around my waist,
as I carried them to bed.

Could that be the cause
30 years later of this excruciating back pain
that's laid me out for nearly three days?

Maybe?
Probably?
Oh, well.

At 50

my gums are receding,
but on the good side –
I've finally gotten a superpower,

Invisibility –
well, at least to young attractive women.
They stare past me

as if I were transparent
and sometimes they walk
right through me. Really.

I ought to remind them of physics,
but that'd be yet another boring suggestion
to elicit nothing but a yawn.

To top it off, the soles of my feet are dry
as the proverbial Mojave.
On a good night I remember

to dab a puddle of lotion
specially made for scaly skin.
All my old flames would confirm my inner snakiness.

What was inside has been made manifest.
And while not too soon,
I hope to slither into that dappled hole

destiny insists awaits all cold-blooded creatures,
tonight I've world enough and time.
Catching a *film noir* flick with my one true love,

basking in front of those blue flames
of that sacred object,
formerly known as the idiot box.

Is there something wrong with me
that off the top of my head,
I can think of dozens of worse places
but not one better?

What a Thing to See

What a thing to see – dead leaves come back to life.
They tumble in an orange, red, and yellow blizzard.

On the ground, they regroup
and rush into the street.
First this way then that,
leaping like a corps de ballet.
They spin, double, even triple plies,
pirouetting on one stem.

Hold your rake,
wait to mulch.
Give slow thanks for the dead coming back to life.

I'd heard rumors of it –
this preacher or that –
but never believed it
till I saw it with my own eyes.

The street's their stage,
And I, dazzled by their wind-powered twists and turns,
stand in awe.

Who knows, but that one day
all this human clatter
will grind to a sure halt.

Every computer go blank,
abandoned cars slowly hollowing out,
tall buildings gone black as tarmacadam,
no human eyes left to squint at *La Gioconda*
in a gloomy Louvre.

But there would still be the leaves,
the dancing, wild, crazy leaves.

Ken the Obscure

I confess – it was I with a twist of wrist
who let go a tangle of fire,
freed the prisoners of the mayonnaise jar.

Freed them to dance their mating dance,
their arcing parabolas,
their upside down tears.

Freed them to shine like cellophane
as they rose on warm thermals
above cirrus and ether.

To rise to the vast void of space
where a pair of Gemini astronauts
would spot them drifting
past their half-moon windows,
like a constellation yet uncharted.

This is where I really should include a literary allusion,
Sinners in the hands of an angry God,
or my Mistress' eyes are nothing like the la, la, la.
You get the drift,
wowing you with my erudition, my over-education.

But I refuse to bowl you over
with lines so obscure,
it would take 10 tenured professors
a month to delineate each phoneme.

Just now my mutt has jumped on my lap.
Her thick fur bristly, her breath foul.
She leans her taut body against me,
and suddenly I forget what I was writing about.

Love Song for the Terminally Maladjusted

Tonight let's make love in the clear moonlight
like young lovers again.
Let's not fret about our sore joints, our saggy bottoms,
the creaking of old bones, even chest pains,
and potential heart attacks.

Tonight let's make love in the full moon's light
like young lovers again.
Gripping firmly each other's
more-than-ample love handles,
let's make love through the night,
or at least, until one of us falls asleep.
Trust me, it won't be long.

Tonight let's make love under the starry night
like young lovers again.
Let's not be embarrassed
by slapping cellulite,
our not-so-taut bodies rippling.

Let's ignore our smells, our twin homeliness.
After all, by this time,
we could very well be six-feet under
or ashes in some forgotten urn.
So let's enjoy, while we still can.
Tonight let's make love like young lovers again.

About the Author

Ken Wheatcroft-Pardue was born in Galveston, Texas. He's an essayist, short story writer, and poet, who survived 25 years of high school teaching. Over a hundred of his poems have been published in such venues as *The Texas Observer, Red River Review, California Quarterly, Concho River Review, Borderlands,* and two anthologies of Texas poetry.

CPSIA information can be obtained
at www.ICGtesting.com
Printed in the USA
FSHW010011261020